# *Saying the Necessary*

## Poems

# Edward Harkness

Design & Composition by Shannon Gentry
Printed in the United States of America
Cover Photograph by the Author
Author Photograph by Devin Harkness


Published by Pleasure Boat Studio
8630 Wardwell Road
Bainbridge Island•WA 98110-1589 USA
Tel/Fax: 1-888-810-5308
E-mail: pleasboat@aol.com
URL: http://www.pbstudio.com


Library of Congress Card Number: 00-100730
Harkness, Edward
Saying the Neccesary / Edward Harkness


ISBN: 0-9651413-7-3 (Hardbound)
ISBN: 0-9651413-9-X (Paper)


First Printing

To Linda, lover and gardener,
who knows nothing grows without
patience and care,

&

to my parents, Harry and Doris Harkness.
Without you I'm nothing.

# CONTENTS

# *Flying Fortress*

# Goldenrod

*—for Linda*

Here is harebell, here the snowy blossoms
of serviceberry. Along the bank's raw edge
foxfire ignites, wild with summer,
rose red as it burns. The smell of sage
brightens an afternoon lit by lupine,
sweetens this sand bar the next flood will ruin.
The Naches glitters on the leaves of an aspen,
colors clouds over Timberwolf Mountain.

From pine shade you step out to meet me.
Heat shivers off the bones of Clemens Ridge.
*Which weeds are these?* I ask. You slip free
from your muslin skirt and spread it on the ledge.
You say *Goldenrod,* and the word takes root
in the sand where we lie, transient as light.

# 1964

This is the room where they found them,
he in the cheap wooden chair, his legs
crossed, head back, the wall behind speckled
with his blood. She lay on the motel bed
in a flowered house dress as if napping,
gloved hands folded on her chest,
the pillow soaked, her blonde hair prim,
hardly mussed, eyes open to count
the acoustic tiles forever. They picked a Sunday.
"Like they just come back from church,"
my aunt recalls. She never replaced
the carpets. My job: to make the beds
all summer for people passing through Bijou
on the scenic drive to Reno, stopping for a night
at the Paradise Motel on Lake Tahoe,
water so pure people pump it straight
to their houses. Leaning over a rowboat,
you can see your shadow on the blue sand
thirty feet down. Behind the chair the stain
still shows where she scrubbed and bleached.
Pets okay. My uncle instructs if coloreds come
I'm to say I'm sorry, I must have left
the vacancy sign on, we're full. My cousin,
who has four years to score some weed,
float through high school, become
a journeyman carpenter with his father,
discover Thoreau, get engaged, design
and build a house, and die in Quang Tin Province,

is upstairs stomping to "I Wanna Hold Your Hand."
No one's home. He's gone berserk.
The hi-fi thumps the walls.
My aunt taught me tuck-and-pull,
sheets folded back four inches.
Three hours a morning, ninety cents.
I have to pay her a nickel every time
I say "huh?" Nights I wash dishes
at Burger Heaven, owned by Carl Jensen,
a beet-faced right fielder for the Red Sox
until a line drive crushed his knee.
He char-broils the patties himself.
Smoke from burnt meat trails across
the highway and onto the lake where
water skiers lean into long glass walls.
Carl has a bat in his office in back, his name
woodburnt on the scuffed barrel. People fool
with Carl, he says, I show them this.
Under the sweatshirts in my dresser
hides a speaker from the Bijou Drive-in.
My cousin popped the clutch in his dad's pick-up,
window still rolled, ripped the speaker
from its stand, cord and all, a story I will tell
for years, as if it meant something big.
In one version Lucy Jensen sits between us,
her pale eyes wide, her fingers tight
on my wrist as a cop chases us, siren wailing,
above the lake, across Donner Pass and down
into Nevada, stars so green and silver
in the incandescent desert air I've begun
to believe I really saw them trace their slow
unalterable arcs. In this version,

I don't scrape grease, fries and gobs of catsup
from heavy white plates, I don't make beds,
I don't check to see if the stain
is still behind the chair in unit #7.
In this version I drive my uncle's burgundy
GTO convertible, I outrun the cops all the way
to Carson City, pull off Interstate 80 where we park
breathless in the dust that follows,
our hearts banging their cage doors,
and we laugh until tears come.
From a saguaro a strange bird cries.
A quarter moon sails and fades.
No one says a word about the speaker,
its black cord torn and dangling.
On the climb back to California the sun
flares in my eyes. At seventeen I'm oldest,
so I let them sleep. The trees change shape,
the light sharpens, and I know I will endure
two lives: one I invent—I give it away freely.
The other I reveal haltingly—even to myself—
in bits and pieces. Sometimes they align
as the same story. Sometimes, the same life.

# Checking the Well

Grampa lowered
the long cord
and bulb.
Way down.
Way down the water
made a perfect mirror.
A boy's face gazed up—
pale moon with a cap.
*Am I that small?*
Grampa smoked. His forehead
glowed like orange wax.
I could almost see inside.
He talked about
levels of water.
*Be kinda thirsty*
*come October.*
An alder leaf
tumbled.
Rings.
Mossy smell.
Flakes of cement went
   *shunk    shunk*
Echo.
If a small boy fell,
where would he go?
Into his eyes?
Grampa held my belt
and I leaned.

## The Night Kid Paret was Killed on TV

Again the sky has gone to seed.
Damn blackberries!
I dodge my way
through Mrs. Roat's orchard,
scratched,
imagining her big dog.

    *Eddie? That you? Door's open.*

Joe watches the fights,
the blue screen, sips an Oly.
Jean stuffs clothes
in the drier. I redden
at Linda's bra
and filmy underpants.

    *Who's fighting?*

Joe says
    *Benny Paret and some other nigger.*

The Kid is trapped in a corner.
Hard right.
Another booming right.
The crowd comes alive!

Linda says
    *You wanna Coke?*

*I don't care. Yeah.*

The Kid's head snaps,
lolls like a doll's.

Solid left, right.

His head shakes No.
Shakes No, no.
No. Seven, eight times.

Loping home, I hear
the moon growl,
caught in the teeth of a dead fir.
I feel my head, the new
soft places,
fists of air slamming
some lovely humming in my ear.

# Helen

I see her tearing strips
from a sheet, tying
sweet pea shoots to chicken wire.
Her hair is Asian, wistful,

teased by April wind.
She sings *Beautiful, Beautiful*
*Brown Eyes,* looks up and winks
the way jaunty women did back then.

That fall her blossoms
withered without her.
Grandma took me to the room
of the dead smell.

Propped by pillows, Helen
grinned, shrunken, the bleached
branch of her leg exposed,
naked to the thigh.

On the bedside stand were pills,
Kleenex and a paper cup.
She fumbled with lipstick,
poked in place the last wisps

of her hair, winked and rasped,
*Hey there, good-lookin'.*
She tried to light a cigarette.
Grandma had to steady

her dangling wrist.
*It's a kick, Erm,* she wheezed.
*Ain't it a kick?*
Red stained her yellow teeth.

What became of the maroon
Schwinn, chrome and cream trim,
I got that Christmas?
Where's the gray slush

I tried to ride it in?
From her kitchen,
Grandma studied the sky's
cold sheets fold and fold.

Sunday forever, forever July.
Morning is a girl's dress
floating over houses, trees.
I tie my own sweet peas

to chicken wire,
lean forward to water them
and enter a room the color
of hospital broth.

*I grew these for you.*
*Let me fill your cup.*
*Helen, why are you dying?*
*Open your eyes. It's me.*

# Right Field

No kid I knew ever hit a really long ball—
to left, maybe, but not to my island,
my abandoned kingdom in right.
I'd pick dandelions,
rub spit in my glove,
study the frayed lacing.
Even then I was waiting for something—
a cloud, rain, a huge crow to flutter
onto the diamond and lift me
beyond the dull ache in my ribs.

They were ahead, no outs.
I dreamed of a warm purple lake and
        *thwack,*
a ball began to rise toward deep right center.
No one knew about my appendicitis,
not my mother, and not my coach,
Mr. Glen Bitterbender,
the first grown man I heard utter,
"Jesus, have I got a hard-on!"

That ball climbed the afterdinner sky,
peaked as a wave surged through me.
Glen Bitterbender bellowed,
"Hustle, you little bastard!"
I sprinted, howling, my gut on fire.
The runner at third waltzed in.
Behind him jogged the guy from second.

In that expanse of parched grass,
my ankle found the lone sprinkler head.

I did this dance of death,
tribal, an insane contortion.
The ball dropped like a meteor,
smacked my left big toe.

I'll never know how I got my glove down there,
never even felt it slap the pocket.
"To second!" the coach barked.
"Throw the damn thing to second."
I lobbed it in on two hops for the double,
and from second the relay and force at third.

Triple play.

We didn't win that game.
We didn't win any game.
After my surgery, Coach Bitterbender
brought me three lemon cupcakes.
Next season he called, his voice cracking,
to tell me I'd been cut.
The season after,
drowsing in his recliner,
sports page draped across his eyes,
his heart tore loose from its worn stitching.

Once again,
through the summer dusk,
high above the backstop,
above the stubby hemlocks along Fremont Avenue,

the ball, my secret star, is rising.
    *I got it   I got it*
And the mothers—not mine—
jump from their folding chairs to cheer
the pale boy they thought too small to play.
They watch me hobble in, nimble,
clutching my side.
My face is a mask.
Pain to me is normal, a way of life.
Glen Bitterbender pats my cheek.
"Sweet, Eddie. Now that was sweet."
I shake my stinging hand and grin.

# Flying Fortress: My Father Survives the War

I imagine the roar as silent
after seven hours in the sky
over Austria or Dresden,
the Forts in stacked formations
of a hundred lumbering bombers
with payloads of five
five-hundred-pounders.

Every airman is certain this is not
the morning white flak exploding
from below or black flak raining
from above will slice a fuel line
or shatter a pilot's face or neatly
amputate an aluminum wing
and send eleven crewmen spiraling
like Icarus crazed by the sun.
If hit, my father had no way out.
His parachute wouldn't fit inside
the turret—his plexiglass world
where he pitched and yawed,
gloved hands locked
on .50-cal. machine guns,
open target for any Messerschmit
flashing through keyholes in the clouds.
They swarmed like bees
one Sunday morning in particular
over Berlin, he 19 and sweating
in his heated suit, the plane pitching,

jolted from artillery, death
from any direction, *fuck,*
after 33 missions, the war
almost over and luck's gone.
See the curved horizon,
puffs of dust five miles below
where bombs hit, a 17 to the left
break in half, no chutes.
*Okay. Okay. Goodbye Mom, Pop*—
the Messerschmits howl as they pass
falling back to pick off stragglers
lost or low on fuel, his own ship
pitching, bombs away like babies cradle
and all, him squeezing the triggers—
Did he hit one?—they gleam like knives—
*Jesus if You love me show Yourself*
the ship turning blind toward the sun
*squeeze the triggers turn you sonofabitch*
specks of sunlight
spiking the fuselage perforated
from bursts of bits of metal.

I will be born and hear these fragments,
how the sky opened once more,
how the German fighters vanished,
scattered by a squadron of Tuskeegee Airmen.
They escorted the 17s home
across the scalloped Adriatic,
above the Alps where ships
on earlier runs went down in fog.
In his red-tailed P-51, one Tuskeegee flyer
pulled aside my father's bomber.

Dad took off his oxygen.
So did the other flyer.
Dad waved, gave thumbs up.
The fighter pilot—a man with kind eyes
is all my father recalls—
nodded, tipped his wings and flew away
as the base in Foggia came into view.

I never asked him did he kill people in the war.
He did. Over the Alps, blocks of ice
spangled like broken blue cities.
In that world above this one
the four Pratt & Whitneys droned.
Up there he glimpsed his savior for a moment—
a man from Alabama—the closest
to a black friend my father ever got.

# Nap

You lie on the made bed.
Dust glitters, suspended
in the room's patient air.
Your body is not dust, not yet.
It's a submerged canoe,
like your father's was—
24 years at Boeing,
years that got him nothing
but a bad back, discs
worn down to chalk,
a clunker Oldsmobile
gray as pavement.
All those fall afternoons
he'd disappear,
nap till dinner, late sunlight
draining from the bedroom,
his head pressed between
pillows to muffle the static
of quarrels, TV, slammed
cupboards, the rasp of traffic
on Aurora Avenue,
and a boy's cracked laughter.

It's your turn now
to nap away an afternoon.
Outside, your sons cackle,
happy as chimps.
Their rusty swings

wail the song of a man
who dreams he's sinking,
the man your mother warned you
not to disturb, the man who,
drifting through filtered light,
wakes to find that dinner
is over, the kingdom of dust
rising before him.

# Burying the Afterbirth

Chill morning.
Sun lurks behind the burned-out barn,
sullen as March,
lobbing a shadow
that parches my cheek.

I lean on the spade—
crunch of leaf mulch
caked with frost.
Devin sleeps, dreams a scarlet roar.
You sleep,
bloom into your father's private plane,
plunging through his final dusk, 1947.

Me, I believe the snail
glides on prayer.
The lily drowns
and never drowns.
I tilt the pail.
Your placenta spills into the ground.
Tomatoes to grow here,
maybe chard.
Back of the shed,
the sun cackles,
reels across a field of fireweed,
splashing light,
and is still.
I fill in the hole.

# Putting Things By

I only know it was Montana, nightfall,
out a long highway,
one of those canyon roads that goes and goes.

We stopped the car, hiked an overgrown pasture
reclaimed by bitterbrush and sage
and entered the listing hulk of a barn.

What year would that have been?

Pigeons fluttered high in the arched rafters.
We held tight.
Our flashlight caught the spray of hay dust.
The last blue of day shone through broken shakes.

Smell of old saddles, bridles.
Smell of old cow shit in empty stalls.

On a shelf thick with the grime of years
we found a Hills Bros. Coffee tin,
a red one,
picture of a guy in a turban.
On the side: "Copyright 1932."
Inside, something hard, tarry, sweet.

I warmed it on the stove,
scraped the black gunk off the top
to reveal the secret of eternity:

honey, dark as molasses,
forty years old and fine.

We ate it on cornbread.
I stirred it in my coffee.
I still believe someone left it there
for us to find—
a farm woman
long dead,
a life of putting things by
—cherries, pears—
in blue jars.
A woman who cared for bees.

We put things by to last against decay.
The barn, the tin, they rise
above a wild field of irises.
You'll forgive me for saying this:
time is honey. Now we glide together
across the Swan Mountains
over moonlit snow.

*A Note to My Sons*

# The Worlds I Know

Don't breathe, I tell my son,
they'll die. We lean over the cold
blue hood of the car, bend close

to watch the first flakes,
small as salt grains,
light and break or stay whole.

I point a numb finger:
Look there, tiny perfect stars,
I say without speaking,

only with my eyes, and he nods,
smiles, shows me one of his—
a palace so ephemeral

it floated here. I wish I had
a magnifying glass. I wish
I had another life to give him

the worlds I know, the worlds
I don't, and together we could
enter the church of a diamond.

I'll have to settle for this:
a logging spur two rutted miles
above Rattlesnake Gorge.

Over a broken pine, just visible
against gray, a red-tailed hawk
traces lonely ovals.

Flags of green moss cling
to a bony snag. He's tall,
nearly as tall as me.

Our lungs give out
and the ghosts inside us rise.
He shivers in bitter air,

says nothing, and I know too
well it's time to move on,
the snow normal now, not strange

lace along the line of hills.
On the quiet ride down, our hearts
whisper from their separate cells.

# My Son's Drawing of a Smiling Deer

On the way home in the car
he crayons it brown as my boot.
It's the doe we saw
near our tent on the sandbar,
flood-raw after the runoff.
From the fat potato body
legs curl like sprouts.
Waxy yellow eyes light her
from within. He gives her
a dainty tail.
       Startled
by our voices on that shore,
the real deer stared,
leaf in mouth, blinked, bolted,
then swam across the river
into trees. The real deer
of my son's vision he graces
with a long smile,
smile of a boy who has seen
something wild return his gaze.
His doe browses in the white meadow
of art paper. No river,
no mountain, no stippled sky.
She is his secret self
brought to light and life,
almost human, almost animal—
a boydeer from the other world.

# His Night Light

                                  glows
in the corner of his room—
a campfire far off in the trees.

Fever burnishes his cheeks.
He wheezes,
puffing out his lips.

Lying with him, I ask
the light:
*Where are the words*

*to draw out his disease?*
Like peonies in a breeze,
his eyelids flutter.

We have survived
the shipwreck by clinging
to a plank,

rocking on the sea
of ragged sleep. There,
far off, the beacon burns.

We are nearing land,
the gray country of dawn,
an island where we can

stay just as we are.
We never have to die here.
Let the waves repeat

their stories. Let these
be the words. We can
cook over a fire

on our secret shore,
the sand cool and blue
forever on our skin.

# Seven Star Spoon

*Qi Xing Xi,* the Chinese say.
Greeks pointed to the Big Bear.
And American slaves
followed the Drinking Gourd.
Tonight the Dipper stands on its handle
above Bethel Ridge, where, today,
through binoculars, we spotted
on a bare slope a dozen black-tailed deer
browsing in gold grass.
Tonight, Christmas, we're out for shooting stars.
Old snow crunches underfoot like toast.

Friends, we've made it this far.
Inside, our kids play blackjack by the fire.
Our kids don't like the bitter air
or understand why we shiver
out here and stare at the deep glittering.
Kids, like winter days, come and go.
Kids, like stars, are always.
We can make out spidery aspens,
hear the river sputter over stones.
They'll be fading soon.
They don't see us tumble
over the ridge toward the Seven Star Spoon.
They don't know we are migratory,
we are headed north.

*—For the Bortons: Rich, Wendy, Brian,*
*Jamie, and David*

# A Note to my Sons

Tonight they're far into the country
of sleep. I read Du Fu's letter
to his son, Pony Boy—
tender confession of a father's pain.

Who knows what business may
suddenly call me away.
I'll be parted from them too,
someday, on a trip of my own,

down Rattlesnake Gorge,
across Goose Prairie by twilight,
where I'll enter, alone
and uncertain, Naches Pass.

So I'll say it now:
I miss you, Ned, Mr. Gray Eyes,
mimic and clown;
and Devin, experimenter, searcher,

you beat me at chess—unforgivable.
Though you're in the next room,
someday the distance between us
will be farther than stars.

# Dragon Kite

# Dragon Kite

*—Tianjin, China*

They gather at the footbridge,
headed to market to buy rice,
a day's potatoes, or
a *jin* of slick black eels.

He arrives in his ancient
cotton jacket, same dark blue
everyone wears, padded, at least,
against a taut March breeze.

Today he brings his dragon kite.
Three boys carry its bamboo body,
down the canal, gently unfolding
its yellow paper wings. Shouting

commands, he feeds out line.
Stooped old women with lily feet,
young men smoking, coasting
on sleek Flying Pigeon bikes,

mothers hoisting the one baby
the state allows—they all
stop to break a day's routine.
He reels in slack, waves, yells,

and the boys let it catch a gust.
His dragon balks, sags, climbs
above the scummy ditch
glittering with glass,

above wires and a stark, half-
built apartment, same shape,
same red brick as the rest,
drab as a government decree.

High against ribbed clouds,
his dragon, fierce-eyed and
undulant, gives its colors
to a chilly morning, blue-tinged

with coal dust. Carrying our daily
bread, we gasp as his creature
leaps, snaps and gallops
headlong into the dirty wind.

# Auden in China


In the '30s I witnessed the depressing dazzle—
the pagodas, the squalor, Shanghai's fetid
Pearl River, and on its banks the rag heaps
of the starved—that stench clings to me still.
Even history reeked, so spiraled, so unwound,
time corkscrewed nowhere, moving and still.
Mao lit out for the tan Yanan Hills,
surviving on conviction and rice gruel.
Later, they called it the Long March—
6000 miles in a single year, one in ten
survived—a retreat so far-flung and complete
it won the peasants and the war.

I only came to meet Du Fu and Li Bai,
those poets in their T'ang boat,
spluttering their poems on West Lake,
drifting aimless toward dawn's mottled skin,
plum blossoms caught in their beards.
Forever an exile, I settled in America, where
natives are aliens but hate to admit it.
We have jeweled lawns and bread lines.
Everywhere you feel the "quiet desperation";
the young country is ancient, naive to its ruin.
God-fearing men plan wars to end all wars.

What became of those drunks who sang
to the moon and back? Legend says they toppled
overboard, tried to cling to each other,

drowned in a net of stars. Legends lie
in the face of heaven. I saw Li Bai and Du Fu
in a pond—white-bodied, whiskered, nosing the weeds.

# Watercolor Painting of a Bamboo Rake

*—by Qi Baishi, 1863-1957*

Nothing can be this plain:
a bamboo rake leaning
against a tree.
Rice paper, Chinese ink—
took ten minutes tops—
a lifetime of observing.
Mr. Yu, my painting teacher,
calls the technique "dry brush."
White space dominates,
as with a poem framed
in its white window.
The handle's a thick
dark swatch, the tines
gnarled, claw–like,
curled in suggested weeds.
The gardener leaned it
there, having neatened the soil
around flowers, maybe,
or a grave. He has worked
in heat and rain, year
and year, has seen floods,
famine, war, all the debris
of history, and still devotes
himself to chrysanthemums.
There is no grave, no gardener
we can see. We make believe.
Qi painted this at 88.
Paper and ink, rake or poem,

something of ourselves lives
in everyday things.
And for all the things not
included in the painting,
not mentioned here, they too
sing in the mind's choir,
in the white space
we can never hope to fill.

# Superman in China

The theater's cold, half full
of kids and their folks
bundled in hats and coats.
Before the lights dim,
we draw the usual stares.
We're foreigners, *Nimen de Meiguo
pengyou*—"We're your American friends"—
and we've come to see the American
Man of Steel, *Chao Ren*, and Lois
glide like gods over Miss Liberty
and the decadent city below.

The dubbing's lovely, Brando's Jorell
intoning like a Chinese Moses.
Then, of course, scenes of crime,
essential to any image of the States.
The Big Bomb goes *boom,* California
comes unglued. Death of Lois.
A grieving Superman reverses
Earth's orbit, reverses time,
saves his secret love
saves us all from doom.

We stroll out to a sooty afternoon,
streets flowing with cyclists,
manic Chinese cabbies in Nissans.
An old man squats by his dozen
geraniums. *Nin hao*—"Hello!"—

we say to his toothless grin,
his eyes a bright forever in the sun.
And for a moment there's no America,
no Superman, just us *waiguo ren,*
"outside-country-persons," chatting
in bad Chinese with this *lao ren*
and his baskets of red flowers,
who's waited for us on his noisy,
tree-lined street in Tianjin
two thousand years.

# Alone on the Great Wall

Slaves built this to keep the barbarians
at bay. Barbaric as the next man, I want to ask
our Chinese guide, whose English is better
than mine, something historical, polite.
Instead, I spy on a river of tourists jammed
thick as Chinooks running the Puyallup.
The Wall loops forever like ribbon beyond
the farthest ridge. The billion stones
a million workers lugged up these mountain
trails must know some ugly stories.

Long steep climb to a tower away from
the horde. Beyond the crenelated gun sights
rolls the enemy's country, a valley
where corn sang in people's bones.
Mongolian wind kisses my cheek too roughly.
Straight down, Kodak film paper wrappers
lie strewn among chunks of ancient mortar.
A giggling Korean boy flings his can of Coke.
Chinese graffiti is etched on every brick.

Green soldiers in dark glasses stroll arm in arm—
maybe killers from Tiananmen.
Two thousand winters ago other soldiers
stamped their feet, dusted snow from black fur hats,
studied those same hump-backed hills. They saw
an icy horizon, clouds of their breath in retreat.

Tourists disappear. I'm alone trudging homesick
toward the next tower with a message
for a sentry from Hunan: *Light a signal fire.*
*Tell the guy in the next lookout to hit the sack,*
*no one's been spotted for days. Tell him we're*
*all foreigners, all afraid of the dark, and tonight*
*the only assault will come from an army of stars.*

# Qin's Clay Army

*—Xian, China*

We believe artists were slaves.
It took an army of faceless craftsmen
to make these larger-than-life soldiers,
each an individual—general, captain,
swordsman—all with brave eyes,
each as real in most detail as us.

We believe artists worked till they died
for the good of the state. Each decided
at the point of a knife, sword or word
to support the regime, help the emperor
fight the long battle of eternity.
If his soldiers won, he'd live again.

We believe artists had their skulls
bashed in to keep the secret from us
visitors from Chicago and Hiroshima.
Their works are an irony older
than Christ, not as old as dust,
for dust is king of kings.
We believe we're free to believe,
admire Qin or hate his guts.
Here's another man who battled
the barbarians of his dreams.

We believe artists knew what they
were doing. No one considered revolt.
All knew they'd be clubbed in the end,

flung in a pit, their grave diggers
also clubbed and flung. No one would
ever know. We think all artists
were slaves. They loved their Emperor Qin
and died like warriors in one man's war
against the one puny soldier Death.

# Music in Tonglou Park

*—Tianjin, China*

Huddled in June shade, they bang their cymbals,
crack their wooden clackers. One in pith helmet,
gray slacks rolled against the heat, pulls a bow
to make his Chinese violin whine, a sound
so strange locust leaves quiver in pain.

The crowd hems them in—widows, street sweepers,
arthritic heroes of the Long March smoking
long-stemmed pipes, a gape-toothed ice cream vendor
pushing his cart, crying *Bingguar yi mao yi mao!*—
they come each noon to sit on stone benches,
fan themselves and listen. Their faces shine,
lined like fine pale soil.

A slender woman hobbles from the shadows.
Waving her coy fan, she sings, her voice
a humming wire, each word stretched to breaking
in falsetto *jingju,* Peking opera style.
She wails some ancient heroic story—
even the vendor falls silent. The listeners
cheer, their eyes glitter with memory.

To grow old...*mei guanxi*...it doesn't matter.
Sunlight hangs in streamers through the trees.
The breeze is polite, Confucian. In a corner
of the park, where the singer's tragic voice
doesn't reach, a girl in jeans and print blouse,

her lipstick redder than Mao's red star,
kisses the boy in designer shades, the one
who taught her to waltz. They're not ashamed.
They do not suffer the past which embraces them.
The singer's wailed words die away.
The lovers hear only their quickening hearts,
the far off *clack clack cymbal clack clack.*

# Shanhaiguan:
# East End of the Great Wall


Here's where stones go back to sand.
Waves assault their flanks and win.
Tourists ignore this place. The Wall
collapses into piles of gray rubble—
nothing for a picture except the plain
pink cherry blossoms on trees below.
Birds I've never seen bank white, cry out
and disappear in the air's blue mirror.

Emperor Qin said build a fortress, one
that never ends. A million prisoners
and working stiffs obeyed the cruel
son-of-a-bitch. Presidents do the same.
Presidents say die for freedom and we do.
They say build bombs to blow the blue earth
away for freedom for America and we do.
Some say the Wall is one long tomb.
One day soon the ghosts of workers will rise—
engineers, masons, cutters, haulers—
and walk these stones again
and send tourists fleeing to their buses.
Below this turret a repair crew mixes mortar.
A high school dropout, a hundred pound
block on his back, struggles up a trail.

The guidebook tells the story of Lady Meng.
Her husband, Wan, was a poet with decadent
bourgeois tendencies. Wan, dreamer and free

thinker, lugged those same hard loads
mile on mile, day on stony day. Winter came.
Snow lashed the Wall and still the slaves
obeyed and broke their butts for the Emperor.
Lady Meng made her way to the construction site
with a padded jacket and fur hat for her Wan.
She searched and searched. Ain't seen
your old man in ages, a worker told her.
Every soldier and foreman played dumb.
She wandered the Wall, her tears like acid
etching the granite where they fell,
till she came here where even granite wept.
The Wall burst open and there lay
Wan's white bones. Wild with sorrow,
she leaped from this ledge into the sea.
The guidebook describes her as "a dutiful
wife, a model of devotion." My tourist map
shows a temple built in honor of Lady Meng.

I'm not Wan. I can't find the temple,
only the curved ledge of the Pacific.
America, country of huge, invisible stones,
I want to swim home to you, or to an island
where all walls end in foam,
where lived no emperors and no slaves
on the windswept shore of my cheek.
On the narrow beach below, Chinese school kids
blow up green balloons, let them go *bzzzt*ing
toward Pan-gu, the Creator, that scowling
figurehead who rants to himself,
locked in his temple in heaven.

# *Black Butterflies*

# Spain, 1938

By the time they lined up the next batch of women
against the stone wall behind the cathedral,
the rain had slackened and bleachers had been
set up. Vendors sold pastries and tea.
Fathers hoisted sons onto their shoulders.
No longer refined, the crowd grew rowdy.
But when the *comandante* lowered his baton,
the women who were about to die, their faces
gray with fear, began to grin. One by one—
first the old, toothless widows, and then those
who were still girls—all lifted their coarse dresses
over their heads, as though they'd planned this
outrage, exposing breasts, thighs, and the dark
wedges of their sex. "Filth!" one father yelled.
He hid his child's eyes. And the well-dressed wives
of these men, they too hid their faces with
their fans. I don't count myself among them,
but some in the squad—boys from small towns
in the mountains—were seeing a woman's secret
for the first time. The *comandante* was furious,
but he never lost control. When we fired,
all the women stood naked before us, arms raised,
their eyes shielded, and their blood flew up
like quail against the wall. Nothing like that
ever happened again. Nobody misbehaved,
except for one old gentleman. He carried on
like a school girl. The *comandante* kindly permitted
him to sit on an empty ammo box and smoke,

his head in his hands, crying a woman's name—
*Marta,* I think it was: *Marta! Marta!*—
while we took aim.

# Lincoln Brigade Reunion

Fifty years ago they hefted packs, ammo
and carbines. Hunched in their folding chairs,
cupping their ears, they lean forward
on canes and listen to The Old Days.
They see again the young faces—
sons of professors and farmers,
daughters of Trotskyites and Wobblies,
see blood splashed on the cobbles
of Barcelona, dead horses on a mountain road.
One frail warrior tells of Freddie from Delaware—
he fell under lemon trees.
And Hannah, the New Jersey painter—
she tripped a German mine and became a rose
opening forever in her father's palm.
Pasionaria sang the sorrow of the ages
to dying Madrid. And Garcia Lorca
of infinite songs, discoverer of the color green—
the *Guardia* led him out in moonlight.
They shot him in an olive grove.
Some of these failing eyes saw Guernica crushed
in an afternoon by Heinkels and Junkers—
"a testing ground," Goebbels wrote
in his diary. Gathered in the cold junior high
auditorium, these heroes of lost causes
try to remember who they were and why.
A young woman helps the keynote speaker
to the podium. He says he's Joseph, he's 87:
*I had this friend...Roberto...lovely Roberto.*

*He played flamenco...I couldn't help him.*
*We left him lying on riverbed stones.*
His quavering voice rises like wind.
*I'm a God-damned Jew! You don't think*
*we knew the meaning of Spain?*
He coughs, wipes his angry cheek.
The woman—his granddaughter, perhaps—
leads him to his chair and only then
the sharp applause from the audience of two dozen.
Children again, these wrinkled soldiers shuffle through
the cafeteria line for grapes, cheap wine
and cheese. The woman folds a table.
Someone's grandson snaps a group picture.
Joseph and a shaky comrade hug and toast
each other. It's Saturday afternoon.
The young janitor, cigarette
on his lip, tuned in to his Walkman,
strolls in pushing a broom.

# On Reading of the Hanging of Benjamin Moloise in South Africa

—*Beidaihe, China*

Here on the Bohai sands
waves curl into their green sounds.
Benjamin Moloise was hanged
today in Pretoria.
Where the sun burns the water
Chinese fishermen fling their nets.
Their boats bob like corks.
Beyond boats and nets, my country floats,
a dream of faraway blue.
Benjamin Moloise was hanged today.
In blue padded jackets, a crowd
of locals comes to stare
from a pier at the weird Americans
in their shorts and bikinis,
leaping in and out of foam.
That old woman with pruny skin
has never seen a blond boy, never heard
an American boy shriek and splash
in the chilly sea we love.
Benjamin Moloise will never stroll
this blond shore. Beyond men
and their nets floats an island
where no one is ever hanged.
On the far end of the beach,
a young woman sits before her easel.
She paints aspens, waves, wind,

boats bobbing like corks,
a dream of faraway blue.
Today in Pretoria they hanged
the poet Benjamin Moloise.

# Black Butterflies

Flakes of ash, they light
on leaves and grass on this bluff
above the Yellow Sea,
not yellow but a dented
turquoise floor, violent
despite a cloudless afternoon.
We've left the guided tour.
My sons discover a notch
on the hillside, a cave closed
by swords of brambles.
We duck and enter the cool dark,
nervous and no matches.
There's a glimmer, a niche,
and beyond—endless blue.
Sentries crouched here, spying
at enemy ships during the occupation.
Old photos show Japanese soldiers
in Nanjing practicing bayonet drills
on bound Chinese prisoners.
From our lookout we spy
white flags of waves
marching in afternoon sun.
We emerge, blinking like newborns.
To our right, Laoshan—Old Mountain—
rises holy and green.
Below, tired Chinese tourists
straggle back to busses.
Here, black butterflies whirl

like bits of paper,
harmless, their occupation
of the hill complete,
the small pages of their wings
chronicling the history
of life and death on earth
in a language lighter than air.

# At the Site of the
# Underground Missile Silo

*—Lincoln, Montana, for Steve Christenson*

1.

Remember how the day ended
in a flash of bright blood?
Just the corny kind of sunset
bad poets adore, and good ones like you.
We left the highway,
drove the quarter mile
red dirt road, stood
in the glare of floodlights
and a tall white totem we guessed
was the monster's guidance system.
The ground hummed.
Something down there snored.
Something down here hissed.
Inside the ring of chain-link
and razor wire shone the hinged lid,
waiting for the day it will fly off
to give terrible birth.
They've buried them everywhere,
you said, all through the heart of the state.
A great white sign glared:
    UNITED STATES GOVERNMENT PROPERTY
   THIS AREA UNDER CONSTANT SURVEILLANCE
        NO TRESPASSING
Dead of typhoid from infected blankets,
ghosts of Sioux children
danced in one gray cloud.

2.

Night brought a delirium of stars.
We wandered away from the glare, the hum.
You named the constellations:
Andromeda, lonely maiden,
chained forever to her ledge in heaven;
Leo, sphinx-like, gazing
at the black riddle of nowhere;
and the Spiral Nebula, twin of our Milky Way,
smudge of light in the attic of space.

3.

It might be lovely, you said,
like all sunsets combined,
a vast morning glory
opening over a city's markets, beggars and birds.
It might be the pure light of knowing
the dying see finally.

4.

Remember JFK?
Missiles in Cuba?
Remember crawling obediently under our desks
hands over our necks?
Mrs. Blandish was blunt:
So that flying glass
won't sever your spinal cord.
Mrs. Blandish, piped one 3rd-grader,
what does *sever* mean?

5.
Steve, all our lives
the earth has been enemy soil.
Now we've become our fathers,
those distant men who read the news
but never talked about it.
What do you say to Kerri?
Yes, life could end?
My oldest son, Devin, says he thinks
he understands.
He plans to build a laser
to make all bombs disappear,
including the laser.
The other night, Ned, his younger brother,
cried out *Mama!* in his sleep,
blubbered a tale of panic,
of running a red road in the sky.
Said it turned black, to quicksand.
A monster pulled him under,
pulled his brother and Mama and me under.
It cracked all our bones.
I held him, whispered It's okay,
Daddy's here, and suddenly I recalled
Black Elk's vision of the good red road
his people never found,
and our red road going dark toward the glare,
the hum I can still feel on my neck.

6.
It's taken me years
of staring at my face
in the window at late hours to learn
that poetry can't teach us to be decent,

can't free the slaves we make
of ourselves. A poem is nothing
but the heart's logbook,
a record of private calms and storms.

Tonight, above my neighbor's sleeping house,
hangs Jupiter, my jewel,
first pointed out to me by you
above that Montana prairie,
a night wild with the smell of sage,
the silo floodlight an unnatural star
behind us.

7.

Remember when earth meant *home, life-giver?*
Let's make a new language, you and me.
Let's learn again the old words,
the old ways of naming before the world
went nuts and brilliant men discovered
how we might all be cremated at once.
Here are words I love: *moss, agate, heron,*
*silver, peach, madrona, curve ball* and *Linda,*
word for the woman I love.
And I love those stars you named, changeless
as hope, knitting together past and future,
same points of icy fire our ancient parents
beheld in wonder in Africa by a stream.

Picture an old woman in some far city
we'll never see. She's tired, her feet hurt,
she loves her one geranium on the sill.
Let her stand for every soul in that city,
city like my Seattle, your Boston,

city of parks, ice cream, sorrow.
Imagine that missile in the foothills roaring.
Imagine the silent brilliant flash,
the woman's face at the window, the geranium,
her last look of knowing.
Imagine reciting the names of every soul
in that city with the unpronounceable name.
Imagine saying *Brother, goodbye.*
*Sister, I prayed it wouldn't be you.*

# Woman with the Egg

*—with thanks to Susan Mieselas, whose story this is*

She comes to you with a single egg,
her gift in exchange for help.
You are in charge here, you are

the Salvadoran colonel in charge
of hunting down *subversivos*—
all young men and women, the priest,

the village teacher, the old man
with one leg who melts down lead
fishing weights and hammers out

bullets all day, one at a time
in his hut for *los muchachos,*
and for his daughter, 14, who left

to join them in hills that rise
green as parrots behind the village,
killed up there with the others—

her name, Blanca Rosa, eyes gouged,
who lies now in the clearing,
her grave unmarked, under corn.

You are in charge here.
Your U.S. Army fatigues hang loosely,
your mirrored glasses made

by workers in Philadelphia.
In them, the world occurs twice:
two dawns, two town squares,

two rivers of rosy light,
two squads of soldiers, M–16s
slung on their backs, milling about

the town cathedral, smoking Marlboros.
She comes to you offering an egg,
tan as her skin. Her daughter is sick.

A lump—an egg-shaped mass—
blooms from the side of the child's head.
There has never been a doctor

in this town. Would you please ask
the good men in San Salvador
to send a doctor for my daughter?

The frightened girl hides
in the folds of her mother's
white skirt. You are in charge.

Overhead, the *whomp-whomp* of a Huey
gun ship terrorizes the air. You stroll
toward your U.S. Army jeep,

made by workers in Detroit,
grab a bullhorn made in San Jose,
where sunrise is a delirious stain

over the city, and you announce
that houses are to be searched,
and no one, repeat, no one will be harmed.

The woman and her daughter have
disappeared. The woman's egg
lodges in your mind like a grenade.

She offered you your life, her life.
That egg was grace. And you,
in charge of this operation,
you refused.

# Kenny Atkisson, KIA, Khe Sanh

I hike the slick ball,
ricochet off Art, the fat boy,
and lope 30 yards down field—
too far for your slender arm—
wave my hands and holler
*Hit me! I'm open! I'm open!*

You skitter, throw head fakes,
scramble from quick Skip Campanili,
dodge a pimply kid we called Beans,
and you loft—Jesus, a bomb!
It climbs the sharp November air,
spirals over the time barrier,

obeys the Law of Falling Bodies,
twists and thunks in my ribs,
knocking out my wind.
Skippy swoops my knees away,
but I'm over the imaginary line
that counts for the world.

Gasping on dead legs, I pick
cinders from my cheek, spit blood.
The others drift off with their
voices into the failing light
of 1964. You saunter to my side—
you're smaller even than me,

your hair braided with sweat,
round salmon eyes raw as rain.
Your blond, high school smirk
is so damned American it can do
anything, whatever in hell it wants.
Once, in Junior Lit., you cued me

from your front row seat.
Pale against the blackboard,
I stuttered my way through
MacBeth's final speech. I froze.
*Idiot,* you mouthed the words,
*...tale told by an idiot.*

Twenty years dissolve.
Your reedy voice rises out of cinders.
From this playground rises
memory of a war that never
made sense. Your words catch me
like a shot to the gut:

*Finally beat them bastards,*
*didn't we, Eddie, didn't we?*
*Nice grab, nice hands.*
Across the open field of death
you sing: *Way to go, Shakespeare,*
*way to go.*

# Rifles

1.
How those killers thrilled me,
looming above Grandma's fireplace,
bayonets in their sheaths,
there with the Christmas cards,
candles, hand-made pine cone wreaths
and two ceramic squirrels.

American-made relics from a lost war,
those rifles rust on nails now in my garage.
Russians used them against Japan, 1905.
In the Solomons, 1942,
Japanese aimed them at GIs.
History always comes home.

She'd pull one down.
At 12 I could barely lift it—
it was taller than me.
I'd seen pictures of soldiers hunkering
through mud or oil or scorched island sand,
the dead washed ashore like kelp.

I'd reverently pull off the sheath.
The foot-long knife still gleamed,
still sharp, its edge nicked by...what?
Along the blade ran a deep groove,
a channel in the bright steel.
That's the blood gutter, this gray-eyed

lover of dahlias explained, who had read
to me *Peter Rabbit, Red Riding Hood,*
and *The Pirate Don Derke of Dowdee.*
She'd ram home the bolt.
I'd squeeze the trigger. *Click.*
The scarred cherry stock

glowed like burnished cordovan.
And what did those four notches mean,
cut with a pocket knife
just beyond the raised sights?
What's it like to shoot and see
a person sprawl? Hours I'd cradle

in my lap this heavy artifact
of family history,
this weary world traveler.
It ended as scrap in a dockside
pile, Okinawa, fall of '45,
Hiroshima and Nagasaki still smoldering.

2.
From alders back of the guest house,
deer would step into Grandma's orchard
to browse on pears, strip the bark
from apple and cherry. Jays would squawk
as if they owned July. A bear
lived in those woods.

I'd lie awake in a top bunk
and listen to rafters whisper,
the rasp of wind in cedars.
I'd lope with my rifle through mud

or oily sand, throw the bolt and fire
at shapes in the guest house window.

Nowhere was lovelier
than Harper Hill in winter.
Snow erased all roads.
With the blue arrival of night,
smoke rose from stone chimneys.
Window lamps cast squares

of light across the drifts.
Inside, the tree she cut herself
bore its tinsel, colored balls
and star. Over the bright fire
hung the rifles, their bayonets
grooved with blood gutters.

# High Country Climb

# North of Orcas

We cut the motor
and let stars take over.
Small waves tapped against
the ribbed wood hull
of our rented runabout.
We sat together.
Our bare arms touched
in the dark.
*Listen,* you whispered,
*A heart beats all around us.*
At that, the surface frothed.
A school of dolphins
had risen,
breaking the ceiling
of their heaven.
They studied us
as children study
with amused sympathy forlorn
polar bears at the zoo.

We considered ourselves—
twenty years married,
floating on the skin
of this life,
watched from everywhere,
by those dark swimmers,
borne by them,
and saved.

# Comet Hyakutake

*—Midnight, Mar. 24, 1996*

What we see up there by the familiar
handle are the trailing gases.
It's just a smudge, a traveler
in an ordinary starry sky.
My neighbor, her breath rising as a plume
of wisdom, tells me we should write out
these cosmic comings and goings
for distant generations—
how we stood on frosty lawns or fields
or drove away from the city's distracting glare
and peered at a new light in the warehouse
of heaven, not as bright as we'd hoped—
a fuzzy wandering eye in the spring of '96,
end or almost end of the Millennium
and a tough century.
It wasn't God who appeared,
furious at our failed world.
What we witnessed was purely mathematical,
a piece of the machinery.
Hyakutake, an amateur, saw it coming—
ice, rock, helium—
trash from the beginning of time.
Just as Comet Hyakutake appeared
and held us rapt with its vague blue,
the first crocuses emerged in a shaded
corner of the garden,
lit their purple lanterns
and ended winter.

# The Man in the Recreation Room

                                      is screaming
again. From season to graveside the moon turns blue.
How unhappy. How his mind moves dreaming

something blue with passion: three wings combing
space beyond a valley. What a view!
The man in the recreation room is screaming.

His hands have a mind of their own. He's palming
a gravestone. The moon has nothing to do.
How unhappy. How his mind moves dreaming

beyond a blue valley. His wings are flaming.
He's afraid his plans have fallen through,
the man in the recreation room. He's screaming.

Past apples, another starlight tries claiming
his eyesight. Lilacs die. All untrue.
How unhappy now? His mind moves dreaming

his hands slowly become his feet. The humming
in his head grows beautiful. Just for you
the man in the recreation room is screaming.
How unhappy. How his mind moves dreaming.

# High Country Climb

*—for Randy and Bill*

From an outcrop,
where trees give way to walls of basalt
cracked by small blue flowers,
we rubbed our sunburnt eyes.
Late afternoon, late summer,
we three men in our forties
sipped whiskey from tin cups.

Back of us,
native cutthroats ringed the surface
of the nameless alpine lake—
a black mirror wedged in crags.
Our tent pitched on a polished
granite bulge, our boots hot
and kicked off, we groaned, exhausted,
felt good, we said,
like the gods we were once,
our shoulders raw from pack straps.

A great shadow crawled across
the valley floor, up the glinting ice
of Mt. Daniel, pink in final sun.

And then we talked—this and that:
how, suddenly, we wished our wives were here.
And our kids, off on their own now.
How tired we were of work routine,
the boss, bills, the broken clutch.
How our lives hadn't turned out

quite the way we thought,
and now what to do with our folks,
aged, growing frail.

The mountain swelled,
the whiskey darkened in our eyes.
We joked about blisters on our blisters.
With the evening chill rose
the piny smell of heather.
That final switchback was a killer.
Yeah. Never again. Never again.

Far off, a trout splashed in heaven.
We stretched on still-warm stone,
remembering how stars can swim—
forgetting for a moment they are only
sparks of ice, the world below is heartless,
and tomorrow we must go down.

# Tossing a Rain-Soaked Journal
# Back in the Burn Barrel

It says here fuchsias droop
like cartoon shooting stars
each July, and the moon is forlorn
this May. It moans along Dry Creek.

March. Frost coats the pines like sleep.
The years withhold information.

Bugs have eaten most of winter.
Just as well.
Whatever you wrote in winter
no longer applies.

For tonight,
stars are self-inflicted wounds.
Tonight, mid-June,
stars are shards of a blue mug
settling in marsh ooze.

On this page the only legible word
is *rapture.*
It might be *rupture.*
*Clouds...No...Clocks...rupture?*
*Loud scripture?*

Most lines bleed off
till they're Chinese characters
in green fog,
crow tracks in melting snow.

This is not the first time
you've resurrected your dead voice,
not the last time you'll discard
what can't be lost.

An evening chill rises off the creek.
One star, already so sharp it hurts,
sings alone on the tin roof
of the chicken coop.

You tear the tattered pages
like yanking wings off moths,
crush a season's worth of mutters
day by day, drop them in the barrel
with egg shells, dead batteries,
an arthritic boot that will never walk again.

Scattering pine needles for luck,
you flip a match and it all goes up—
your lost language in which *fuchsia*
stands for everything you love.

Beyond the brief hem of light,
you are illuminated to scavengers, nocturnals,
a mother skunk and her brood.
They lick your cheek with their eyes.

# Tonight

Before me—papers, a dry pen, three empties
and something that, years ago, might have been
a ham sandwich. Tidbits I call "My Life."
I wish I could say, *Before me—hills pleated*
*and tan, a doddering barn spreading its one*
*good wing of morning shadow, cottonwoods,*
*wild irises waving, a chestnut mare chewing*
*her singular vision of dusty grass.* I want to say
*Night. Snow.* Long for sparks to whir from a campfire,
become stars, flutter down as black
blossoms, as tiny extinct birds.

But no. Only this clutch of clutter before me.
Kids are down, Linda drowses, her novel
toppling off her chest. I stay up to catch
the late news and watch flies dance in the nostrils
of starved, ghost-eyed children, whose faces
are moonscapes, desolate. Then the ad for toothpaste,
the one that gives your breath a fresh, minty taste.
Then the faces again. I switch the channel
and there they are, dying a second time.
I twist the color adjustment till their reed–like arms
burst into blue-green flames, then I flip off
the whole vicious world, sick, wanting to growl,
retch, gouge my cheek with a fork, wanting to crawl
bare-kneed down a road of crushed glass
and out of this life.

Here comes the last bus
from town. A hunched, hatless man steps off gingerly,
in pain apparently, cradling a bundle close. A baby?
He stands there in his stolen coat, his shoulders
already spotted with rain. The bus slips into
one of the dark crevices just beyond
the city limits. I turn out my desk light.
He doesn't know I can see him. But the bundle—
why do I want to say it's a fiddle?—
he holds tightly to his chest. With every step
he takes on the wet street, a blue rose
blooms and fades. He approaches my door.
I see his head is deformed, like a boy I recall
from the fourth grade, who couldn't talk,
only moan and drool. We had no idea how brilliant
he was, how he would later predict the locale
of certain invisible stars.

In his crooked way, the man trudges back
into shadows, and I realize there is no
shambling man—I've been gazing for an hour
at my mailbox, half-hidden by a shrub.

So let me say this. A man has placed a fiddle
wrapped in a gunny sack on my porch.
There it is, before me. And even though it means
waking Linda, even though children starve
and cannot utter a word, I plan to learn to play
my fiddle—crudely, of course—tonight.

# Cliff Above the Yakima

No one drives
the canyon road today. Today
is an evasion. The Yakima
trembles in slow flashes.
Today tries
to stop flowing.
I fling a stone, watch it
scissor air
and disappear. The river
soaks it up
like a wavy mirror.
Daisies flake
the rock, hills bend
with blue afternoon.
I wad my shirt,
toss it, watch it flutter—
blind white hawk. Toss
my shoes—
they weren't happy, would've
left me one night anyway.
Two nickels glitter
in the sun.
Whatever sinks will surface
in another poem.
Whatever floats will
migrate to the sea.
I hear my ballpoint
pen hit rock

and shatter, ink
discoloring the water,
water the color
of the world, all
I throw away.

# Kaylyn, Hermiston Elementary

Thanks for the plastic ring, Kaylyn.
Your dress is a rag, absurd,
your scuffed oxfords four sizes too big—
idiotic relics from the sweet
dead America of 1955.
Your eyes are flecks of flint
from Tennessee,
have squinted more than once
into a dark unnameable.

I picture your mother gaunt,
your father harsh with vise grips
in his greasy fist, haunted,
hunting you,
beating a rusty fender in the ravine.
During geography,
you doodle, drifty,
you sketch me handsome,
a gentle mouth,
a smile I wish I could wear.
The teacher—a depressed soul—
speaks aridly about yearly rainfall in Paraguay.
*Precipitation,* she says, and smiles.

You pound the red ball
against the bricks in the vacant
school yard till dark.
During lunch the secretary whispers:

"Don't be charmed; Kaylyn'll steal you blind."
Tells me they sent you out west to Hermiston
to live with Aunt Rachel, who feeds you
but seldom washes your hair.

I still hear the older girls cackle.
You caught me in the hall at lunch,
your face red as the ball you slam,
and stammered:
"You wrat such perty wards."
You poked the ring into my hand
and I went blank, as I'm known to do.
In shame, you scrambled into the crowd.

I leave my car to stroll the river road.
It's less a road,
more a badly healed scar.
The Umatilla spills color back to clouds.
Day decides to die with dignity,
igniting the riffles.

Kaylyn,
your gum machine ring fits my little finger.
One meadowlark trills so loud
he opens a wound in the evening.
The blandness of his feathers
gives his song its pain.
Kaylyn, if I were handsome,
you'd be lovely as your name.

# Cutthroat

How many hours
have I stood gazing?
Light pools behind
a green boulder.
They lurk there,
undulant as moss,
their red gill slits
open and close
like heart valves.
Shadows on the hill
say it's afternoon.
I've cast and cast,
the line chirping
to that smooth spot
where the hiss
of upstream rapids
doesn't reach.
I want to bring one home—
a muscled horizon
in my hand, black moons
from nose to tail.
Everything is luck,
and that's why I come:
to hear rocks accept
the steady wash of time,
to lose track of it,
to believe there's
something deep

and alive out there
just beyond my lure,
something I'll never own.

# Winter Wren

The cat drops him at my feet—
a mangled feathery nothing,
the short tail quivering oddly.

And whatever I'm doing—turns out
I'm under pressure, today's
the deadline—I stop,

cup my hands and bear
this walnut-sized wad of lint
outside. He teeters forward

on his needle bill, dying,
I'm certain, his head bent—
the last beat of a bruised heart,

BB eyes blinking toward
whatever he imagines forever is.
I place him on the shore

of a puddle in the drive.
He sways, stands, more alert now,
eyeing me, beak open,

panting like a boxer
at the final bell. I study
his brown speckles—not

what you'd call a pretty bird:
stump-colored, gray rump,
twig legs—and I leave him alone

to survive his own deadline
at the edge of icy water.
His head twitches, he shakes,

hops in his pond, then out,
and flutters off as if nothing
has happened, as if the world

is not out to kill you
when your back is turned,
when you think you're safe

in the shadows, completely
nondescript, camouflaged,
hidden in the leaves.

*Saying the Necessary*

# Saying the Necessary

I read of a Montana man
whose pickup
stalled in the mountains.
Cross-country skiers
found him next spring,
their skis rasping
on the top of his cab
just showing through the snow.
His engine dead, no map,
he'd apparently decided
to wait for help.
His diary calmly records
his life of being lost.
He describes the passing days,
how he rationed his crackers,
an Almond Joy,
built a few small fires at night,
ate his emergency candles,
ice from a pond,
a pine's green lace of moss.
He hoarded every spark
from his battery.
There's evidence he wandered
up a nearby ridge.
He might have noticed a marmot,
gold and relaxed on a rock,
or spotted mountain goats
wedged high in gray basalt.

From a pinnacle of broken
lichen-colored scree
he watched the world bend away blue,
rivered with trees.
He might have heard
the whine of a plane
in the next valley,
looking, looking.

Then the cold came.
Frostbite settled the matter
of hiking out.
He wrote detailed accounts
of the weather,
noting the clear, icy air,
little flares of stars
drawing no one's attention.
*Not so frigid this evening.*
A later entry read:
*Ribbed cirrus clouds moving in.*
Then brief goodbyes
to his wife and daughter—
*my lilac, my rose.*

When the blizzard buried him,
he wrote by his interior lights,
and when the battery failed
he scratched in the dark
a strange calligraphy,
covering the same pages,
the words telegraphic,
saying only the necessary
as he starved.

In the end,
his script grew hallucinatory—
*...toy train... ...oatmeal...*
*...farmhouse lights just ahead...*—
illegible, finally,
like lines on a heart monitor.
Several pages he tore out and ate.

He must have known
even words wouldn't save him.
Still, he wrote.
He watched the windshield
go white like a screen,
his hands on the wheel,
no feeling.
He listened to his heart
repeat its constant SOS,
not loudly now,
but steadily—
a stutterer who's come to love
the sound of his one syllable,
at peace with his inability
to get anything across.
He must have pictured himself
wading through the drifts,
traversing the heartbreaking distance
between voice and any ear,
searching for tracks,
a connector road that leads
down to everyday life.
By glow of moonlight filtered
through snow-jammed windows,

his last act was to place his book,
opened to a page marked Day One,
on the passenger seat beside him.

# About the Author

Edward Harkness grew up in Seattle's north end and has, with a few exceptions, including a year's teaching stint in the Peoples Republic of China, never gotten very far away from home. He holds degrees from the University of Washington and the University of Montana; at the latter he earned an MFA and studied with poets Richard Hugo and Madeline DeFrees.

His poems have appeared in many periodicals, including *American Review, Poetry Northwest, Seattle Review, Fine Madness, Portland Review, Northwest Review,* and *CutBank.* He is the author of several chapbooks, including **Fiddle Wrapped in a Gunnysack** (Dooryard Press, 1984) and **Watercolor Painting of a Bamboo Rake** (Brooding Heron Press, 1994). **Saying the Necessary** is his first full-length collection.

He teaches writing at Shoreline Community College and lives with his family in Shoreline, Washington, which is an easy bike ride from his old north Seattle neighborhood.

# ACKNOWLEDGMENTS

Some of these poems appeared in the following:
*AfterNoon: An Online Journal of Poetry and the Arts, American Review, Arnazella, Chariton Review, Crab Creek Review, Crosscurrents, Ergo!, Fireweed, Hand Prints, Jawbone Broadside Series, Northwest Illustrated Arts Paper, Poetry Northwest, Portland Review, Seattle Voice, Seattle Review, Spindrift, Switched-on Gutenberg* (an on-line journal of poetry), *Tailwind, Talking River Review, The Poet and the World,* and *Mudlark* (an on-line journal of poetry).

Other poems first appeared in the following chapbooks:
*Long Eye Lost Wind Forgive Me,* Copperhead Chapbook,
      Copper Canyon Press, 1975
*Fiddle Wrapped in a Gunnysack,* Dooryard Press, 1984
*Watercolor Painting of a Bamboo Rake,* Brooding Heron Press, 1994

And still other poems were anthologized in:
*Where We Are: The Montana Poets Anthology,* Lex Runcimen and
      Rick Robbins, eds., CutBank/SmokeRoot Press, 1978;
*Rain in the Forest, Light in the Trees: Contemporary Poetry from the
      Northwest,* Rich Ives, ed., Owl Creek Press, 1983;
*Strong Measures: Contemporary American Poetry in Traditional Forms,*
      Philip Dacey and David Jauss, eds., Addison–Wesley
      Publishers, 1986.

I wish to thank Artist Trust for awarding me a GAP grant, and Shoreline Community College for giving me a sabbatical leave. The grant and the time off from teaching have made it possible for me to finish and publish *Saying the Necessary.*

# Other Pleasure Boat Studio Books:

William Slaughter, *The Politics of My Heart*
(ISBN 0-9651413-0-6) $12.95 • 96 pages • Poetry

Frances Driscoll, *The Rape Poems*
(ISBN 0-9651413-1-4) $12.95 • 88 pages • Poetry

Michael Blumenthal, *When History Enters the House:
Essays from Central Europe*
(ISBN 0-9651413-2-2) $15 • 248 pages • Nonfiction

Tung Nien, *Setting Out: The Education of Li-li,*
translated from the Chinese by Mike O'Connor
(ISBN 0-9651413-3-0) $15 • 160 pages • Fiction

Irving Warner, *In Memory of Hawks,
And Other Stories from Alaska*
(ISBN 0-9651413-4-9) $15 • 210 pages • Fiction

## Chapbooks from Pleasure Boat Studio:

Andrew Schelling, *The Handful of Seeds: Three & a Half
Essays*
(ISBN 0-9651413-5-7) $7 • 36 pages • Nonfiction

Michael Daley, *Original Sin*
(ISBN 0-9651413-6-5) $8 • 36 pages • Poetry

# Orders

Pleasure Boat Studio fulfills orders placed by telephone, fax, e-mail, or mail. Response time is immediate. Our discount schedule is universal. The same discounts are available to individuals, bookstores, and libraries.
2-4 books, 20%. 5 or more books, 40%.
Free shipping on pre-paid orders.
Send check or money order to:

**PLEASURE BOAT STUDIO**
8630 Wardwell Road
Bainbridge Island•Washington 98110-1589
Tel-Fax: 888.810.5308
E-mail: pleasboat@aol.com
URL: http://www.pbstudio.com

Terms and conditions: standard to the trade and available upon request. SAN: 299-0075

**Pleasure Boat Studio Books & Chapbooks
are also distributed by:**

Small Press Distribution: Tel 800.869.7553 • Fax 510.524.0852
Baker & Taylor: Tel 800.775.1100 • Fax 800.775.7480
Koen Pacific: Tel 206.575.7544 • Fax 206.575.7444
Partners/West: Tel 425.227.8486 • Fax 425.204.2448
Brodart: Tel 800.233.8467 • Fax 800.999.6799
Ingram: Tel 800.937.8000 • Fax 800.876.0186

from *Pleasure Boat Studio*
an essay written by Ouyang Xiu,
Song Dynasty poet, essayist, and scholar,
on the twelfth day of the twelfth month
in the *renwu* year (January 25, 1043)

*I have heard of men of antiquity who fled from
the world to distant rivers and lakes and refused
to their dying day to return. They must have
found some source of pleasure there. If one is not
anxious for profit, even at the risk of danger, or is
not convicted of a crime and forced to embark;
rather, if one has a favorable breeze and gentle
seas and is able to rest comfortably on a pillow
and mat, sailing several hundred miles in a single
day, then is boat travel not enjoyable? Of course,
I have no time for such diversions. But since
'pleasure boat' is the designation of boats used for
such pastimes, I have now adopted it as the name
of my studio. Is there anything wrong with that?*

Translated by Ronald Egan
THE LITERARY WORKS OF OU-YANG HSIU
Cambridge University Press